SURVIVAL
OR EXTINCTION

SURVIVAL OR EXTINCTION

*A Christian Attitude to
the Environment*

BY

HRH THE DUKE OF
EDINBURGH

AND

THE RT REV MICHAEL
MANN

MICHAEL RUSSELL
FOR ST GEORGE'S HOUSE
WINDSOR CASTLE

© St George's House, Windsor Castle 1989

First published in Great Britain 1989
by Michael Russell (Publishing) Ltd
The Chantry, Wilton, Salisbury, Wiltshire
for St George's House, Windsor Castle

Typeset by The Spartan Press Ltd
Lymington, Hampshire
Printed and bound in Great Britain
by Dotesios Printers Ltd
Trowbridge, Wiltshire

Designed by Humphrey Stone

ISBN 0 85955 158 X

BAIN CLARKSON
INTERNATIONAL INSURANCE BROKERS

Production of this book has been sponsored by
Bain Clarkson Limited

Contents

Preface

Over the past three years, a series of seven consultations have been held at St George's House on 'The Christian Attitude to Nature'. A list of those who have attended these gatherings is at Appendix B. Whilst the responsibility for the joint authorship of this book lies solely with us, it could never have been written without the scholarship and contributions of many of the participants in these gatherings at St George's House. The first part deals with the history and development of our environment, and the impact that the activities of man have had on that environment. It outlines the dangers that face us and suggests that, until people of all religious persuasions come to believe that remedial action is not only necessary and expedient, but right, little effective action is likely to succeed.

The second part of the book is a development of the many contributions that have been made in the course of the seven consultations. As a result, the authors would not wish to claim that the contents are their original work, and indeed, the participants will recognize how much their individual contributions have influenced the final result. We would, however, accept full responsibility for any deficiencies that may be found therein.

The third part provides some illustrations of practical problems, culled from the experience of those who participated in these consultations, applying to them the theological insights which those participants have drawn from our discussions.

Finally, this book is attempting to tackle a problem that has only recently claimed attention but will undoubtedly be a continuing subject of discussion, concerning every one of us now and of vital importance to future generations. It outlines the dangers that face us and suggests that people of all religious persuasions, or none, should be looking for remedial action. Change is not only necessary and expedient, it can be right and must be made possible if a state of hopelessness and cynicism is not to prevail.

Philip

Michael Manu

Introduction

Scientific and technological advances in the present
century have given humanity an awesome influence on
the world's biosphere. It has often been for the worse, in
war and destruction. It can also be for the better, in helping
to resolve some of the crises which we face. Christians
cannot deny or abdicate the influence which they have
acquired. But Christians believe that all authority belongs
ultimately to God, and they recognize their own fallibility
in making decisions. Are they ready to recognize their
own need for repentance and forgiveness for the way in
which humanity is managing the world, and do they have
the humility to face the facts and to learn to work with the
processes of nature rather than exploit them indis-
criminately only for selfish human advantage?

In 1986 The World Wide Fund for Nature celebrated its
twenty-fifth anniversary at Assisi, made famous by its
association with St Francis. The idea was to link the
secular movement for the conservation of nature with the
religious perception of nature as the creation of a supreme
being. While the delegates discussed the social, economic
and scientific imperatives, leaders of the five major
religious groups – Buddhist, Christian, Hindu, Jewish and
Moslem – were invited by the Franciscan Order to discuss
their separate institutional attitudes to God's Creation.
The anniversary celebration ended with an inter-faith

ceremony in the Franciscan Basilica. The symbolism of this remarkable event made a deep impression on all who witnessed it and on the many more who heard the radio broadcast. Such was the reaction that it was felt that the initiative could not be allowed to rest there. It was, therefore, decided to form a loose association under the title of 'The Network of Conservation and Religion'.

It is bound to take time to divert humanity from the dead end of ruthless exploitation to the path of conservation and sustainable use, but it is hoped that this association between WWF and the major religions has begun the process. It has already given rise to a number of significant developments, particularly in the production of educational material and in the linking of ceremonies and festivals with the theme of human responsibility for God's Creation. One such initiative was the organization of a series of consultations at St George's House at Windsor on the general subject of the Christian Attitude to Nature. This book is a summary of those consultations and it is intended to revive the sense of spiritual unity between abstract theology and the sacred relationship of all Christians to the source of all life on earth.

Christians believe that what God has created is good. It is His intention for His Creation to be good, but what have we humans made of it? The problems that arise are the direct result of human activity and include a whole range of specific threats to the future of the Earth. Essentially they are the problems of excessive population and expanding economic growth. They lead to the depletion of natural resources, the breaching of the ozone layer, the greenhouse effect, acid rain, urban sprawl, the destruction of the rain forests, the pollution of land, air and water, the spread of deserts, the destruction and loss of animal and plant species, the disposal of waste, the increasing demand for all forms of energy. There is a growing awareness of the seriousness of the totality of all these problems, and the fact that no part of the world can escape the consequences. These issues affect every man, woman and child and the very well-being of our planet Earth itself, and the urgent need to face up to what we humans are doing to the Earth must lie heavily on the Christian conscience.

From the earliest times human beings have had an awareness of the 'holy' in that which surrounds them in their daily lives. It has always been recognized that the social stability of any society depends upon a whole range of customs and standards of behaviour, which are intimately related to moral and religious belief. These beliefs have been refined over the centuries by the great religious leaders and thinkers. Sadly, the current age of materialism has undermined this human spiritual awareness, and has helped to weaken the moral motive to care for the natural environment.

The arguments of self-interest and self-preservation are powerful, but they often lack emotional or spiritual appeal. Consequently most significant human advances have occurred when humans have been inspired by a higher motive which they have believed to be right. People in more affluent countries have adopted a life-style which is consuming our renewable natural resources at rates faster than they can regenerate. At the same time development aid to the less prosperous countries is an encouragement to similar patterns of consumption. So there is a need to strive simultaneously for what is just for the human community and for what is sustainable in the natural world. This means a challenge to Christians in the affluent countries to tackle problems on a global scale, and to recognize that our own way of doing things is part of the problem. It also means a challenge to the global community to seek not simply to conserve and protect natural resources but also to work for their regeneration and renewal.

The issues are extremely complex, and the identification of solutions requires scientific evidence, which can take years to collect and interpret, while the difficulties continue to grow. There are no simple panaceas. Generalizations can be dangerous, misleading and counter-productive.

However, Christians have a duty to think through their attitude to the whole of God's Creation, and to be clear about the principles which they believe should motivate the search for solutions. Discerning such principles will then illuminate the general debate which should guide policy makers and help individual Christians to behave responsibly.

We recognize that Christians comprise only some twenty percent of the world's population and that of these the majority now live in the poorer areas of the world. We realize that this book has been the result of deliberations by those of us who live in some of the most affluent countries and we are very conscious of the need for a proper humility.

Humanity is faced by a fundamental conflict between a need for economic growth, to ameliorate the vast problems of the poorer areas of the world, and the need to protect and conserve the dwindling resources of our planet. It is very difficult to combine what is just and what is sustainable, but it is not an impossible task, as the *Brundtland Commission Report** illustrates; especially if Christians in the more affluent countries, sustained by the

---

Report of the World Commission of Environment and Development, set up by the General Assembly of the United Nations in 1983. Chaired by Mrs E. H. Brundtland, Prime Minister of Norway.

basic hope of their faith, are prepared to reorder their priorities and to rethink what is meant by 'growth'. The enormous growth in material prosperity requires a corresponding moral and spiritual growth. The fruit of scientific knowledge and technological advance should be acknowledged as a gift from God, but a gift which requires a corresponding growth in wisdom in order to safeguard it and use it aright. Happiness and contentment do not automatically increase with material prosperity.

.

PLANET EARTH

.

PLANET EARTH

The Beginning

THE beginning was a Big Bang and it is estimated to have taken place between ten and twenty thousand million years ago. Evidence suggests that the universe is almost certainly still expanding, and that all its parts are moving away from each other. The inferred time it takes for the signals from the furthest observed sources of emissions to reach us from outer space implies that they are bringing information about the universe as it was hundreds of millions of years ago. By using such information reaching the earth from outer space, it is possible to postulate what may have been happening to the universe since the instant of the Big Bang.

Over thousands of millions of years, the particles from that explosion are believed to have gathered into galaxies and star systems. About 4,500 million years ago, in one part of the vastness of the universe, among millions of similar bodies making up the galaxy of the Milky Way, a system of planets gathered round a minor star, which we know as the Sun. One of those planets happened to be exactly the right distance from the Sun for stratospheric and atmospheric envelopes to develop around it. These in turn allowed a reasonably stable temperature and climatic system to be generated. There was also just enough water on the planet to ensure the stability of the cycle of evaporation and deposition in the form of rain and snow. At some stage in this process, and by means not yet fully understood, life began.

Man Appears

Charles Darwin had been struck by the fact that, while fossil remains showed many extinct species of animals and plants, they also showed some that appeared to be similar to species still alive on earth. He concluded that these must be related to each other and that some sort of dynamic process was occurring in nature to account for the differences between them. In his *Origin of Species* he developed a theory of evolution whereby primitive organisms evolve into more complicated species and better adapted to their habitat and environment. He proposed that this adaptation took place through a process of natural selection, in which those individuals that were more successful at breeding and rearing young had an advantage over the rest. Under this theory, the species *homo sapiens* gradually evolved from more primitive ancestors over a period of many millions of years.

Since his time, more of the fossil record has been exposed and in *homo erectus* it revealed a 'near-man' that walked on two legs. More fossils of other species of 'near-men' have been found in Africa in recent years, but at the moment the exact relationship between them and the living species of *homo sapiens* is a matter of considerable controversy.

The physics of the solar system and the chemical interaction between Earth's climate and crust with the developing biosphere allowed life to emerge from the oceans and to evolve into more complicated forms. Life continues through a mixture of several functions. Symbiosis, where some species of animals, and some species of animals and plants, can only survive in close partnership with one another. Predation, where predators depend on one or more prey species. Competition for food and habitat, which ensures that a balance is kept between populations and resources, except when there is a population explosion such as the locust swarms in Africa. Specialization, where, for example, different species of small birds feed exclusively on seeds, grubs, insects or nectar.

By what path *homo sapiens* came to be a tool-user and omnivore is not known in any detail, but our species is part of the living world and we depend for our survival on the same complex inter-relationship between the physical structures and systems of the solar system that maintain climatic stability, and the biological systems that provide our food. All these together provide the resources which we use for our comfort and convenience. The healthy state of that complicated inter-relationship is, therefore, vital to the future of our own species as well as to the future of all life on Earth.

Every living organism needs an input of nutrients for survival. Almost all plants derive their nutrients from the soil and water and from the atmosphere. All animals derive their nutrients from plants or from other animals. In general terms, the size of the population of a species depends on the availability of its source of food and the quality of its environment. If a population grows to such a size that its demand for food is greater than the sustainable supply, there is an automatic feedback. Lack of food results in starvation and probably in disease as well, and the size of the population, and therefore the demand, is brought back into balance with supply.

In the animal kingdom there are carnivores and herbivores, scavengers and cannibals, and some are omnivores which enjoy a varied diet of fish, flesh, insects fruit and nuts. It seems probable that the earliest hominids belonged to this latter group. In every animal species the satisfaction of hunger depends on killing some other living creature or organism. One of the very few species to keep and breed other species in captivity to satisfy his hunger, and to use the by-products for his convenience, is man.

However, in spite of his domestication of food animals, man is still the world's greatest predator of wild stocks. Even the whales are no match for him. The so-called game animals, such as deer, wild duck, pheasants and partridges, are taken in relatively small · numbers, but fleets of highly sophisticated commercial fishing vessels sweep the oceans and are currently taking some eighty million tons annually. It is estimated that this global total is very near to the maximum sustainable yield from the world's oceans. This means that if the catch continues to increase, there is a risk that the yield from some species will gradually decline and that others will become extinct. Not only could this source of food be seriously diminished, the whole future of the fishing industry would be threatened.

Many primitive peoples depend for their food entirely on wild stocks of animals, vegetables, fruit and nuts derived from the natural forests. Even among the more sophisti-cated communities there are those who still enjoy the hunt for food by shooting and fishing. In both cases they are concerned to 'conserve' their prey species so that there will always be a surplus to take in the following year. Farmers do the same by maintaining breeding herds and flocks and only selling off the surplus production.

Not all wild stocks are taken exclusively for food. There is a lively demand for the skins, furs, feathers, tusks and horns of wild animals for clothing, decoration and other purposes. Of the immense total catch of sea-fish, a large proportion goes to make fertilizer for domestic crops and feed for domestic animals. The problem about the conservation of wild stocks that are hunted illegally by poachers or that are subject to unrestricted commercial exploitation is that they are effectively 'free-for-all'. As Aristotle pointed out a long time ago:

What is common to the greatest number gets the least amount of care.

This applies particularly to wild marine stocks in the oceans outside territorial waters. It also applies to wild animals with a market value, which then become the target for poachers. In both these cases there is no advantage to the fishing industry or to the poachers to attempt to conserve the stocks. It is a commercial business and what one fisherman, or poacher, does not catch is likely to be taken by another. To make matters worse, the market dictates that the price of any desirable commodity increases with its scarcity. As the numbers of elephants and rhinos in Africa and Asia decline, so the price of horn and ivory rises and with it the inducement to the poachers and merchants.

To give an idea of the dimensions of some of this trade, the following is a quotation from *Traffic Bulletin* published by the Wildlife Trade Monitoring Unit.

The import of CITES Appendix I and II psittacines (parrot-type birds) into the UK may have involved as many as 20,000 birds a year over the period 1981 to 1984. This total can be compared with imports of the same species into Japan in 1981, estimated . . . to have been over 100,000 birds, and into the USA over the period 1980–84 which averaged over 225,000 birds.

It is not easy to estimate what might be a sustainable number of such birds that could be taken from the wild as

[23]

there is a wide variation in the population 'pool' of each species.

It is theoretically possible to reduce supply by reducing demand, and this is the principle of CITES – the 'Convention on International Trade in Endangered Species'. The difficulty in practice is to persuade the consumers not to demand such species or their products. Considering the sheer size of the world trade in wild species and their products and the fact that there is always an unscrupulous element in any trade, reducing demand is not quite as easy as it sounds in theory. Where the demand is for food, the problem becomes even more difficult. As the human population increases, so the demand for food increases and any attempt to restrict supplies to already under-nourished communities is almost certainly doomed to failure.

Continuity and Extinction

The continuity of life is assured by its ability to renew itself through a process of reproduction. Every species needs to be able to maintain a viable population if it is not to become extinct. For the purpose of breeding, many species require resources in addition to food with which to construct their nests or shelters. In the case of the human species, the demand for such resources is relatively very much greater for each individual, compared to any other species, and its power to acquire such resources has become almost unlimited. So much so that there are a number of areas in the world which at one time supported a rich variety of vegetables and animal life, but which, thanks to over-exploitation by the human species, are now deserts. Parts of Central America and South East Asia, Mesopotamia, Persia, the Indus Valley, Asia Minor, and

North Africa, all sustained successful human populations at one time. Today some are complete deserts, or semi-desert peopled by a few nomads, others have simply been abandoned and have reverted to jungle.

The fossil record shows that over the ages a great many animal and plant species have become extinct. The record does not tell us exactly what caused their extinction. Some may have destroyed their habitat by over-population, but others may have been made extinct by a catastrophic change in climatic conditions or by some other natural disaster. We do know that in modern times, the human population has caused the extinction of a large number of species, in some cases by direct exploitation, but more frequently by occupying or destroying their habitats. As the human population continues to grow and as its demands for space and resources increase, so the rate of extinction of wild species is also bound to increase.

The degree of inevitability.

The Human Impact

If you look at the situation of planet Earth from a detached scientific point of view, it is immediately apparent that there are three factors that dominate its future. The first is the increase in the human population. In *The United Kingdom Response to the World Conservation Strategy* it states unequivocally that '. . . the pressure of people is the force above all that makes conservation necessary'. ①

The second is that progress in science and technology and in human living standards is creating a constantly growing per capita demand for natural resources, both organic and inorganic. The third factor is that, while human demand for economic growth in order to maintain – if it is not possible to improve – its standards of living is infinite, the natural economy of Earth is finite. ② ③

[25]

∴ it can either come back into balance catastrophically or through price control or man uses his ingenuity to exercise control.

One measure of the sum total of human activity on this planet might be the output of carbon dioxide gas. A recent article in *The Economist* described the situation like this:

The fields and forests and plains of the earth shelter in an invisible bubble – the earth's atmosphere. The walls of the bubble are getting denser; since the middle of the nineteenth century, human activities have boosted the amount of carbon dioxide in the atmosphere by a quarter. Carbon dioxide traps heat that would otherwise escape into space and as a result the world has warmed up by half a degree centigrade since 1850. This is the Greenhouse Effect.

Regular monitoring of the concentration of carbon dioxide in the atmosphere was started in Hawaii in 1958 when the concentration was 316 parts per million. In 1987 it was measured at 350 ppm. It is estimated that once the concentration reaches 400 ppm, the atmosphere will have returned to a state it has not been in for 1 million years. It is estimated that this figure will be reached within the next fifty years. What effect this will have in the short term is not fully understood, but it is an example of positive feed-back and there is little doubt that it will have a very dramatic effect on the world's climate in the long term.

The question is, just how much battering can the earth's natural system absorb? Does it just gradually run down, like a fly-wheel; or will it take so much before breaking, like a stick? Whatever the answers, there can be little doubt that mankind has been putting it under increasing strain.

The Population Factor

The only way to give an indication of the scale of the population factor is to use statistics. In 1800 the population of the world was about one billion people. It took one hundred and thirty five years (1930) for the population to double to two billion. It then took only thirty years (1960) to add another billion. Twenty years later it had reached four billion. In other words, the population doubled in just over fifty years. By 1987 it had reached five billion, and it is still growing at 1.7% per annum and is expected to reach six billion by the end of this century.

The disappointing fact is that, in spite of the wonders of science and engineering, there are more people living at subsistance level today than ever before in history. Excluding the more affluent parts of the world, instead of the same number of people living at a higher standard, there are four times as many people living at much the same standard as before. The damage this has caused to the ecology of the sensitive areas of equatorial Africa is only too obvious.

Quite apart from the damage that the rapid growth of the human population is doing to the natural environment, it is causing almost insoluble problems for many of the poorer countries in the provision of adequate housing, water supplies, food, schools, hospitals and, above all, employment.

Just to illustrate the enormity of this problem. The total population of India is expected to grow from 607.3 million in 1975 to 1,013 million in the year 2000. This is an increase of about 60% and this means that the urban population will increase threefold.

The implications are frightening. In health care, for example, to achieve the standards by the year 2000 which the more developed countries had reached in 1975, the number of physicians in India will have to increase by 419%, the number of hospitals will have to increase by 117%, and the number of hospital beds will have to go up from 336,777 in 1975 to 4.4 million.

In contrast, the following is a quotation from a recent speech by Mr Mosese Qionibaravi, the Deputy Prime Minister of Fiji.

In the 1960s we were able to significantly reduce our rate of population growth through family planning. This has been an important factor in the modest standard of living we have thus far achieved. If our population growth had not declined after 1960 our total population, currently just under 700,000 people, would have been now 25% larger. The influx into the labour force would be 50% larger between now and 1990. The number of new jobs that would have to be created annually to absorb the increment to the labour force would be some 80% greater than is actually the case.

Clearly at a time of adverse economic conditions and rising unemployment we would now be facing a disastrous situation.

The immediate consequence of the massive world human population is the growing exploitation of the world's natural resources – renewable and non-renewable. Tropical forests are being exploited at a rate far faster than they can possibly regenerate naturally or even by replanting. Some 80% of all known, and still unknown, species of plant and animal have their habitat in such forests. Once the forest goes, the species go with it. Furthermore, we do not know what effect the disappearance of the forests will have on the chemistry of the atmosphere.

The dilemma is that most of the destruction of the forests is caused by the expanding human population looking for somewhere to live and plant its crops. In Amazonia 80,000 square miles of forest were destroyed in 1987 alone. Most of the timber just goes up in smoke, only some 10% is cut for commercial purposes and export to the more prosperous countries.

All this is happening in our time, but it should not require much imagination to speculate what might happen in the future. To quote from the Brundtland Commission Report:

. . . the world's human population may be expected to stabilise during the next century, depending upon when 'replacement level' fertility rates (slightly over two children per couple) are reached. If this rate is reached in 2010, the world population will stabilise at 7.7 billion by 2060; but if it is not reached until 2065, the population will stabilise at 14.2 billion in 2100.

It might be reasonable to add that at the present rate of exploitation there will be no natural forests left by that time and precious few fish in the seas. — The importance of the land
— Fish farming.

The Science Factor

Human communities from the very earliest times have used their abilities to think. In some cases they have specialized in religious and philosophical matters, in other cases the development of agriculture; the study of the heavens or of mathematics; the pursuit of war and conquest; the creation of great works of art and imagination; and some, notably the Chinese, have displayed a special talent for invention.

However, it seems that it was the Arabs and Europeans who developed the concept of science, or the systematic study of observed phenomena by experiment and induction. This allowed good strides to be made in the understanding of natural phenomena, but it caused considerable conflict with traditional knowledge 'inspired' by religious texts. Copernicus, Galileo and Darwin each suffered for daring to suggest that traditional understanding did not always fit the observed facts. On the other hand, the explanation of phenomena provided by science made it possible to predict the behaviour of natural systems and of materials and structures, and from this knowledge came the ability to manipulate natural systems and to design machines and products of all kinds and for all purposes.

This was naturally seen as a great triumph of human ingenuity and a welcome contribution to the welfare of humanity.

And so it would have been, but for unexpected and unintended consequences. Developments in medicine and hygiene and the increase in the production of food have dramatically improved health standards and the expectation of life and reduced infant mortality. This has resulted in the massive increase of the human population. Big human populations and increasing prosperity make demands for more construction; more housing, and more factories, more leisure areas, more roads, more airfields, more reservoirs, and more extractive industries. Every such development further reduces the undisturbed space available for the rest of the living world.

In its single-minded pursuit of progress, humanity is making a far greater impact on the structure and systems of this planet than any other living species. Not content with occupying every available piece of land, all too often we then make a mess of it.

The development of organized industry and the growth of cities, power generation, agriculture and human waste are major producers of noxious effluents which pollute the land, the air and the waters faster than the natural systems can absorb. The demand for more food and more natural resources by the growing human population has increased faster than the earth's limited ecosystem can replenish. Refrigerators, air-conditioning plant and aerosol sprays using fluorocarbon propellants are damaging the ozone layer in the atmosphere and the increasing output of carbon dioxide is causing a rise in ambient temperatures.

It is silly enough for us to destroy our own environment, it is nothing short of criminal to do so much damage to the environment of the rest of the living world as well.

It now seems that science and technology have helped to create a situation which is becoming progressively more difficult to repair. Only greater awareness and understanding coupled with a change in attitude and real determination can hope to halt and reverse the process of self-destruction.

Carl Jung, the psychiatrist, wrote:

> Western man has no need of more superiority over nature, whether outside or inside. He has both in almost devilish perfection. What he lacks is conscious recognition of his inferiority to the nature around and within him. He must learn that he may not do exactly as he wills. If he does not learn this his own nature will destroy him.

Children
?

Increasing Demand – Finite Resources

The earth can only produce so much 'income' in the form of renewable resources. The fact is that the planet cannot get any bigger; the forests cannot grow any faster; animals cannot reproduce and mature more quickly; the climatic system cannot produce more rain to supply the increasing demand for water. Consequently, all further growth in human demand for resources other than food, has to be met by exploiting the earth's 'capital', or mineral, assets. However this latter option, even though it could be done more efficiently than at present, is only open to the more technologically advanced communities and to those fortunate enough to have such assets within their boundaries. For the less favoured, the future is bleak. They are more dependent on living resources and, in many cases, their biological habitat is sensitive. As the population grows, so the demands for renewable resources increase faster than can be sustained, and productivity inevitably begins to decline.

[31]

This process is taking place before the eyes of the world in Central and East Africa. In fifteen years of droughts and below the average rainfall, the human population increased by a third and, to make matters worse, the population of domestic flocks and herds increased by the same proportion. The natural pastures have been damaged and the demand for fuel wood has reduced the tree cover, which in turn has caused soil erosion and the siltation of rivers. It may be possible to help the human population, but it is much more difficult to prevent the spread of the desert.

Food is the most important resource for any species. Modern science and technology produced what has come to be known as the 'Green Revolution'. This has raised the gross output of agriculturally produced food in tropical and sub-tropical countries throughout the world. However, the growth in the human population in many of these areas has meant that the food available per head of the population has not increased, in fact it has declined. Furthermore, the economic growth in those areas, in spite of massive economic – as opposed to conservation – aid programmes, has not been sufficient to improve the social infrastructure. Indeed, some aid programmes have encouraged the ruthless exploitation of natural resources at the cost of incurring huge foreign debts.

More people are illiterate, poor and hungry. Per capita, there are fewer schools, hospitals and houses, while unemployment and under-employment has increased. On top of that, it is now evident that there are not sufficient natural resources, renewable or non-renewable, to provide the present number of the human population with the average standard of living enjoyed by the more affluent communities.

Conventional wisdom suggests that all social problems

can be solved by economic growth – growth of the Gross National Product. The difficulty is that no one wants to admit the obvious, that economic growth cannot be sustained indefinitely in a steady-state ecosystem. It should also be evident that it is impossible to have any kind of sustained economic growth while the ecosystem is in decline.

It may be unpalatable, but it is hopelessly misleading to describe the poorer countries as 'developing'. The sheer size and speed of growth of their populations has made it virtually impossible, even for the lucky ones, to do anything more than to maintain their present low level of living standards. The prospect is that as per capita resources decline, the gross number of poor will increase still further. There can be little doubt that giving greater attention to the conservation of their natural renewable resources would alleviate some of their problems.

There has been much comment to the effect that the rich countries are getting richer while the poor are getting poorer and that this is somehow due to an unfair economic system. Apart from the unequal distribution of resources and the relative resilience of natural environments, it is more likely to have been due, at least in part, to the fact that the populations in the more developed countries ceased to grow some years ago and that consequently any economic growth has raised average wealth, whereas in countries with a high population growth rate, any economic growth has merely allowed more people to survive.

The Conservation of Nature

It was the realization by naturalists that certain familiar species of plants and animals were becoming rare and that others were becoming extinct, that gave birth to the modern conservation movement. In 1948 a group of natural history societies formed themselves into the International Union for the Conservation of Nature and Natural Resources. It has since grown to a membership of about five hundred government agencies and non-government organizations.

The first and very natural reaction was to try to save threatened species from extinction, and in 1962 The World Wide Fund for Nature was founded with the object of raising money for this purpose. WWF is still involved in this activity, but meanwhile much more has been learnt about the reasons why certain species are nearing extinction. It soon became evident that the trouble lay in the progressive destruction and degradation of their habitats and whole eco-systems. In addition, it was realized that the natural renewable resources needed by man were also at risk, and that ultimately all humanity would be in danger.

There are three aspects to conservation:

1. Actions intended to conserve the human environment, but which have little or no significance for the conservation of nature and other living species.

2. Actions intended to conserve the global environment that is critical to the survival of all life on earth.

3. Actions intended to conserve the habitats and integrity of wild species of animals and plants that appear to have no direct value to the human population.

In a way, conservationists are following a well-established technique. In the old days, miners used to take canaries down the mine to warn them of the presence of noxious gases. When the canary fell off its perch, the miners knew that they were in danger. The present accelerating rate of extinction of species suggests that the human environment is becoming decidedly unhealthy. The trouble is that this evidence is only apparent to specialists, and their warnings are too often taken as prophecies of doom. Prophets have never had popular messages, but it is usually forgotten that their prophecies are always conditioned by the proviso 'unless you do something about it'.

There are three obvious reasons for being anxious about the future and for the need to prevent any further damage to the earth's biosphere. There are the social consequences ① of the over-crowding of the human population; there are the economic consequences of over-exploitation of wild ② species, and there are the less tangible consequences of the reduction in biological diversity through the loss of ③ species, including the rapid disappearance of potentially interesting and valuable plants and animals, many of which are not even known to science.

There is also another factor. The development of intellectual powers has allowed humanity to give expression to an awareness of a spiritual dimension in our relationship to time, place and space. To this day, many communities consider as sacred anything from the heavenly bodies to individual trees and springs. They recognize good and evil influences and accept that the viability of their community depends on certain customs, taboos and standards of behaviour. Over the centuries, this spiritual dimension has been gradually refined and given coherent substance by the great religious thinkers and leaders. It is now only too evident that the materialism of the modern age has deeply confused human spiritual awareness and it has obscured the religious and moral imperative to care for what God has created.

Although the events described in the early chapters of the Book of Genesis may not be a factual account of the beginning of the world, anyone with a religious belief accepts that the Creation of the universe was an act of God and that it still depends on God. The compilers of the Book of Genesis say that God was pleased with His work of Creation, therefore if we believe in the existence of God, there must be a moral obligation to care for the whole of His Creation, and not just for that part which is of immediate benefit to humanity. In other words, there is also a moral factor in our relationship to our planet and to all the elements that make up the biosphere in which we exist and on which we depend for life.

The recitation of the environment and ecological problems that appear to be threatening the future of life on earth may seem like a sorry tale of gloom and doom. Gloomy it may be, but doom is not inevitable. There are good reasons for hope. Humanity is quite intelligent enough to be able to respond to the problems. The means are available, only the understanding and the will to act are lacking. What is needed is a wider awareness of the true state of affairs, a realistic understanding of the facts of the divine Creation and, above all, a sense of moral obligation to care for our planet Earth.

THE CHRISTIAN ATTITUDE
TO NATURE

THE CHRISTIAN ATTITUDE
TO NATURE

THE moral basis for a balanced Christian attitude to any set of circumstances, in addition to knowledge and an understanding of the facts, has always rested upon, and has had to be capable of being tested against, three factors:

1. The authority of the Scriptures.
2. The experience of the past as seen in the tradition of the Church.
3. The appeal to individual reason and personal experience.

The moral principles thus evolved form the basis for a code of ethics which guide our actions.

THE AUTHORITY OF SCRIPTURE

We start with the difficulty that many of the environmental problems which we face today were not apparent at the time that the books of the Bible were written. Indeed the pressures that have led to increasing environmental concern have been more cultural than religious.

However, even in Biblical times, human activity was already in the process of causing damage to the natural environment. Asia Minor, Mesopotamia, North Africa and the Indus Valley were either becoming, or had already become, man-made deserts. It was the very success of the civilizations in those areas that brought about the over-exploitation of the soil and of the natural forests, in order to satisfy the growing demand for food, building materials and fuel. It is probable that the degradation of the soil, and the disappearance of the forests took place slowly, and doubtless it never occurred to any one generation of inhabitants that the decline of their civilization had any link with the decline of their basic natural resources.

There are numerous references in the Bible to the right use of the natural order, but they apply to a world where the natural order appeared to be timeless. Today the situation is very different. The face of the earth is changing so quickly that most people over the age of fifty are aware of a change in the natural environment since their youth. This is true even in the least affected countries. Pollution, population growth, the disappearance of natural forests and the extinction of plants and animals have all become matters of discussion and comment, greatly stimulated by coverage by the media.

Christians have always had to cope with new situations. It was cultural pressure that led to the early Councils and the formulation of the Creeds, and it was dissatisfaction with the established order that led to the new insights of the Reformation. Christianity is a dynamic force and the truth of the Scriptures has constantly unfolded and revealed fresh ideas. Christians have always found that when they approach the Bible with new questions they have been able to find helpful answers.

This does not mean to say that all change is evil or harmful. As will be seen it was only later in the Old Testament that poverty, deprivation and hunger came to be seen as evil, and even then it was more as a result of inequalities of distribution than being evil in themselves. There was not such a clear view of our responsibility to the natural order. All things were created by God, but there was little attempt to explain or think through some of the dilemmas, injustices and even cruelties inherent in that natural order.

Christians are now being challenged to search for an answer to the question, whether the present changes are part of God's purpose and are ordained from the beginning, or whether only those changes for which humanity is responsible are against God's will and, therefore, evil. We have to work out the morality in Christian terms, whether these changes are good or evil.

Although this book approaches the subject from the Biblical attitude towards Creation, there are clearly many other ways in which an approach can be made.

The Old Testament Concept of Creation

If Christians wish to draw valid conclusions from the experience of the great monotheisms, Judaism, Christianity and Islam, all of which derive their concept of creation from the Old Testament, account needs to be taken of the way in which the ancient Hebrews arrived at that concept and the imagery in which they expressed it.

Once the idea of the Creator God was accepted, it was natural for those Hebrews to place their stories about the making of the world at the beginning of the long record of their experience of this God. This has conveyed the notion that the first thing they knew about God was that he made the universe.

The concept of the 'Creator God' also encouraged the idea that the world was created specifically for the benefit of mankind. This, however, is the very reverse of how the religious tradition, from which the great monotheisms have sprung, came to its understanding of God the Creator. The Hebrew tribes knew him first and always as God their Deliverer. Before ever they thought of their God as the God of all humanity, or as maker of all things, they knew him as the divine saviour and guarantor of their community to whom they owed grateful allegience.

The behaviour of the tribes fell far short of their ideal, but the dream lived on in the visions and vituperations of their prophets and the value judgements of ordinary people. It can be summed up in the word *shalom* which has a much broader significance than 'peace'. It means the harmony and order of a caring community; the wholeness that includes every aspect and every corner of ordinary life; the balance of interests whereby every person and every creature has its adequate space and its due boundaries in an ordered whole. The balance was derived from a communal awareness of the God who had intervened on their behalf. Their relationship with him was primary.

Throughout the social regulations in which the idea of *shalom* was embodied runs the refrain: 'You shall fear your God and your brother shall live with you.' Servants and slaves were to be regarded as members of the family household. So too were aliens and immigrants. 'You shall not oppress him. He shall be treated as a native born among you. You shall befriend him as a man like yourself because you were aliens in Egypt. I am the Lord.' The same consideration for the existence of a fellow creature is extended to domestic animals: the beast that pulls the plough or the harvest waggon earns the right to graze on the edges of the field. Even creatures of the wild have their place in the sun: anyone finding a bird sitting on eggs may take the eggs but not the sitting bird as well.

The principle that emerges from a multitude of minute regulations is that of the limits set by considerations for other existences within the whole. There is a word in the New Testament that sums up the ideal of *shalom*: not *eirene*, 'peace', though that translates it, but *epieikeia* which means toning in like a creature that has evolved a coloration to match its habitat, or like a piece in a jigsaw puzzle that fits in to its right place where the design links it to its neighbours. So it is used to denote moderation, fairness, reasonableness.

The vision of *shalom* was more honoured in the breach than the observance while the Hebrews remained in possession of the land which had inspired it. It is the paradox of all religion that it becomes most dynamic when its original concept has been uprooted from the soil in which it germinated and to which it still seems to refer. The Hebrews' dream of *shalom* became an idea of universal significance when they were in exile, or drifting back to a homeland under foreign control. So they told of the act of creation in the language of their own deliverance from captivity. God was represented as calling the Creation out of a chaos of darkness and water just as he had called their nation out of Egypt, and through the waters into a new land. As they had been separated out from a polyglot multitude of slaves and given their own place and possession, so Creation is described as a sequence of separations and allocations – light divided from darkness; waters divided from waters and given their proper places and bounds; seas divided from dry land, day divided from night. It is an ordered universe, just as theirs was supposed to be an ordered community. Indeed, the existence of order presupposes a condition of community or interrelation. To deny or ignore mutuality is the beginning of reversion into chaos and meaninglessness.

The image of God the Creator is a powerful one. It provides a reason for the existence of Planet Earth, and for the human presence among a diversity of other animal and plant life. However, as scientific research and inquiry expanded knowledge, it appeared that what had once been inexplicable and incomprehensible, except in terms of divine intervention, could now be given a rational explanation. Consequently, God's act of Creation seemed to be removed from the dynamic evolution of spiritual consciousness to those areas where human knowledge was still imperfect, to the earliest origins of the universe. Such thinking can lead too easily to a 'God of the Gaps' theology.

The Creation account has also led to the misinterpretation that Christians have placed upon the command to mankind to have dominion over the earth, and to be fruitful and multiply. These injunctions have been interpreted in such a way that the future of humanity itself has been put at risk. Christians have been inclined to see the human race as the most important part of nature, and the rest of creation there for its personal benefit. With their unique powers of speech and reason leading to increasing knowledge, which has been applied with great technological skill, humans have hardly needed any further encouragement to see themselves as the centre of creation. Unfortunately, knowledge without wisdom, and power without responsibility, is a certain recipe for disaster.

The truth is that the dominion accorded to man is derived from the likeness to God. It is still God's dominion. Man has only the authority to co-operate in the on-going work of creation. The ability to stand back and to see the Creation as a continuing process, and then to participate in the struggle to achieve perfection, should be seen

Steward

[44]

as a gift to share with God. This is a concept which, rightly understood, embraces scientific inquiry, technology, poetry and worship.

Order versus Disorder

The Old Testament story of the Fall is fundamental to man's understanding of God. It speaks of the human relationship to the natural environment, rather than to disobedience in Paradise. The close inter-relationship between humanity and nature is emphasized. It warns that rebellion against God, and the manner in which He has ordered the world, disrupts both relationships between people and between humans and nature. God has created an order where beauty and righteousness will be established in a system of relationship. When we respond positively we enjoy the blessing of that order; when we disobey, ecological disaster is to be expected.

God made the earth to be fruitful, and Christians should see themselves as God's agents in maintaining and enjoying that fruitfulness and must recognize and respect that they are circumscribed by God's design and breach God's created order at their peril. There are certain things they may not do, and still remain the free agents they are meant to be. The temptation of the serpent was the suggestion to human pride that dominion is personal and that in life and death they are answerable to no one but themselves. This is the hubris of the story of the Fall.

The Creation story in Genesis has a theme of order which God executes in a kingly and majestic manner. Mankind's behaviour is ordered to mirror that of God as a wise and just ruler who governs his subjects in peace and moral order, which is but a reflection of God's cosmic order.

[45]

The whole Creation exists for God's 'pastime' and is not made for man. Humanity shares the world with all of God's Creation, and so has no right to exploit or destroy, for the word 'replenish' contains within it the need to restore and to conserve. If we believe that we are responsible to God, who made all things, then we have a duty to all things.

The Old Testament continually makes the point that sin is not merely a matter between humans and God. Sin alienates our human nature, not only from God, but also from God's other creatures. Salvation involves integration into the harmony which God has ordered for the whole cosmos. Human sin is seen as disobedience and disorder which inevitably brings its own nemesis.

The Old Testament also deals with images of disorder. In Genesis chapters 6–8, the world is purged of evil in order to restore that which is good, and so the flood is a parable of both warning and hope. This hope was reinforced by God's covenant with Noah in Genesis, 8–17, symbolized by the rainbow, and this was not just with Noah, it was 'with every living creature'. Exploitation in any form is seen as sin. In Isaiah 14 and 24, in Ezekiel 28 and Psalm 82, rebellion against God may result in the disorder of God's Creation.

The earth is also polluted under the inhabitants thereof, because they have transgressed the laws, changed the ordinance, broken the everlasting covenant.

The Scriptures are less clear about some of the inherent dilemmas within the natural order. If God is the Creator, He must have created the dangerous and unpleasant aspects of His Creation as well as the good things. Dangerous creatures, viruses and diseases that afflict man, beast and plant life pose a problem. Are they too to be considered as beneficent? Predation and cruelty are part of the natural order. Are Christians doing God's will if they interfere with the natural order when it seems to operate against human interest? If God has created the conditions within the physical structure of the world which are capable of causing 'natural disasters', is humanity doing God's will in trying to prevent such disasters from happening?

If we do intervene, what may be of benefit to some can often be evil for others. What should be the Christian attitude to the experimental use of animals for laboratory experiment? Clearing the rainforest in South America may be causing irreversible long-term damage to the atmosphere and destroying the animal and plant life of the forest, but the farmers and ranchers will see it as good for themselves and their domestic cattle.

It is not sufficient for Christians to adopt a simplistic approach to God's Creation. We are constantly challenged by its very complexities and by the difficult moral dilemmas of cost and advantage which have to be balanced.

Justice and Wisdom

Later in the Old Testament the God-appointed guardians of order were the kings. Solomon asked God for 'an understanding heart to judge thy people, that I may discern between good and evil'. I Kings 3, 9. He was to rule with justice and righteousness, a word which could also be understood as correctness. I Kings 4, 29–33,

And God gave Solomon wisdom and understanding beyond measure, and largeness of mind like the sand on the seashores, so that Solomon's wisdom surpassed the wisdom of all the people of the east, and all the wisdom of Egypt. He also uttered three thousand proverbs; and his songs were a thousand and five. He spoke of trees, from the cedar that is in Lebanon to the hyssop that grows out of the wall; he spoke also of beasts, and of birds, and of reptiles, and of fish.

It is Solomon's knowledge of the natural order in creation that is emphasized.

Isaiah 32 confirms this vision of the ideal king, which is one that maintains the order that God has ordained.

A king shall reign in righteousness, and princes shall rule in judgement,
Then judgement shall dwell in the wilderness, and righteousness shall abide in the fruitful field.

So mankind is seen as a fellow creature in symbiosis with the rest of Creation, where he has no right to exploit or destroy, but where his kingly status imposes upon him duties to conserve the order of all Creation, for which he is responsible and answerable to God.

Throughout both Old and New Testament times, life was very uncertain. There were good years and bad, there was famine and plenty. When crops prospered it was a sign of God's blessing on those who obeyed and followed his design. It was in later times after the establishment of the Davidic monarchy that the Prophets start to detect the emergence of an unjust society, where what was available was not being shared. Isaiah and Amos in particular were not unduly worried by personal wealth, but you were in trouble if there was a starving man at your gate! The prophetic vision was not limited to sharing and distribution, the land itself deserved a sabbath, the seventh year of rest, just as the poor had a right to glean the fields after harvest.

The Prophets also began to emphasize a growing sense of enhancing the quality of life. Isaiah, Jeremiah and Job speak of God as the potter, shaping and fashioning humanity to his purpose. But an enemy wrestles against God's purpose, and the Fall casts its shadow over all human endeavours; Amos's basket of ripe summer fruit is turning rotten whilst they prepare to eat it. Modern science and technology has given mankind overwhelming powers of management and stewardship, which is how the writers of the Old Testament would have us understand the position. Given wisdom and foresight, the opportunities for good are unlimited, but the risks for disaster are tremendous, when there is an inadequate vision to inspire us.

The Wisdom literature is rooted in experience. The wise writers could not have conceived of the possibility of any reality not connected with God. 'The fear of the Lord is the beginning of wisdom' – Proverbs 9.10, Proverbs 1.7, Proverbs 15.33, Psalms 111.10, Job 28.28. It was a wisdom that was grounded in humility. Job's 'comforters' believed that God must punish the bad and reward the good, and so they were judging God by human standards and denying God the liberty to act as He sees fit. God, in Job, chapters 38–40, makes it clear that there is much that is beyond human understanding. God exists for His own purposes. The whole of nature exists to show the glory of God, which is why so many people react to wild beauty with a feeling of closeness to God, for we are allowed to share in God's own pleasure in his creation, for 'It is very good'. Humanity has always been conscious of the wonders of nature, and awed by the immensity of the heavens. The writer of the Book of Job puts words into God's mouth that reveal the depth of his awe and his sense of insignificance in the face of the power and magnificence of the creatures and natural events which are described with such brilliance.

The Wisdom literature makes it quite clear that there is a difference between knowledge and wisdom. Knowledge in itself is amoral, it is the way in which knowledge is applied that is important. Knowledge has to be combined with understanding, experience and the fear of God before wisdom is achieved. Today the cultural environment is dominated by scientific knowledge, but that knowledge is not always applied with understanding either of the short- or the long-term consequences. Species of animals or plants may be endangered, or become extinct because there is not always a full understanding of the reason why they are threatened, or how such adverse results might be avoided. Wise decisions require not only knowledge but also understanding.

For the writers of the Wisdom literature the search for wisdom was the same as the search for God. If there is any quality that Christians need in the search for a better perception of their situation within the living world, it is for the wisdom to understand God's will, so that the knowledge we have acquired can help us to make the right decisions and take the right actions.

The New Testament

In the New Testament it is in the very person of Jesus himself that we see most clearly the union of the 'natural' with the 'divine'. Jesus showed a harmony with nature and a sensitivity towards it; he constantly used the imagery of the natural world to illustrate his teaching. Perfect obedience to the will and purpose of God is rewarded by a divinely ordained harmony between man and God, and between man and nature. It is through our response to the Gospel message of love and salvation, and the consequent mending of our ways, that salvation can come to all

Creation. So Christian attitudes to God, to our fellow men and to nature all interact, and to disrupt these relationships is sin. We cannot hope with impunity to combine an attitude of respect and sympathy towards our fellow men with an attitude of domination or neglect towards the natural Creation.

The modern preoccupation with 'rights' received short shrift from Jesus. In the Parable of the Good Samaritan, Jesus turned the lawyer's question, 'Who is my neighbour?' right round by his own question, 'Who proved to be neighbour to the Samaritan?' The lawyer was really asking, 'Who can be said to have rights upon my "love"? What has a right to my concern and thereby expect my charitableness?' But Jesus shows that such preoccupation with defining the rights of others will always end up by limiting one's own responsibility. It becomes, in fact, as it was in this lawyer's case, a means of qualifying and circumscribing the otherwise boundless demand of the 'second great commandment'. And the more responsibility is confined within conditions and limits, the more the rights of others are diminished. To start out trying to define rights is to end up reducing them. It reduces them to the measure of our own fallen perceptions as to what kinds of people we are prepared to accept as neighbours, and as to what degree of responsibility we feel towards all things. The two 'greatest commandments' of the law are in effect God's 'Universal Declaration of Human Responsibilities'.

Jesus took bread into his hands and blessed it, and broke it, he took wine and blessed it, and gave it to his disciples saying that the bread and wine were his own body and blood. Christians are commanded ' to do this in remembrance of me'. We are called to come to terms with the mystery of the spiritual and the material, the immanent and the transcendent, and to heal the rift between the two.

It is a healing that can only be achieved by first taking upon ourselves the very weakness and wounds of the sufferer before we diagnose the ill and seek for a remedy. The Eucharist demands both a thanksgiving for Creation, and a sharing in it.

The Prologue to St John's Gospel (John 1.1–14) states 'all things were made by him, and without him was not anything made that hath been made', and that if 'the law was given by Moses, grace and truth came by Jesus Christ'. The law must by definition set parameters, but love knows no boundaries. Ephesians I speaks of the way in which all things are summed up in Christ, 'the things in the heavens, and the things upon the earth', and that we are sealed 'unto the redemption of God's own possession, unto the praise of his glory'. In Romans 8.18–25, St Paul talks of the whole Creation as an integral part of God's purpose, waiting to be delivered from the bondage of corruption into the liberty of the glory of the children of God. In Colossians the natural law is seen as a rationalization of God's sustaining power. Salvation is for all life. The Christian approach to the environment is to be one of responsibility and not exploitation; pollution is the effect of man's estrangement from God, and is a measure of his rejection of spiritual values.

The central message of the New Testament is that God is love. God so loved His world that He gave His only begotten Son, Jesus Christ. There are many aspects of this love, but two of the most significant are altruism and compassion. Jesus pointed out that 'Greater love hath no man than this, that he lay down his life for his friends', and there can be no greater challenge to human altruism than this. Whereas the concept of man created in the image of God to have dominion over the earth encourages an anthropocentric and selfish view of our world, the idea of a loving God raises our eyes to a much higher level, and encourages us to have a positive concern for the whole of Creation, even if it means making sacrifices for the good of various aspects of that Creation.

Humanity may be motivated by fears of survival, but Christians must think beyond human survival to the love of the whole of God's Creation. Our motivation springs from a love of God and, therefore, of all His works, combined with a deep and humble awareness of our potential to do harm to God's Creation. We often do not foresee the long-term effects of our actions. What in the short term may seem very desirable can have unfortunate consequences. Transgressing the natural law may bring its own nemesis, and humans do frequently have to learn moral and spiritual truths the hard way. This is not to imply a vindictive God, any more than does killing yourself by jumping off a tall building. The natural order does lay down a cause and effect.

Throughout the New Testament there is a sense of urgency – of crisis – that the end of the times is upon the young church. With the passing of the centuries that sense of urgency has been lost, but it is still an essential part of the Gospel – we do not know the time, and the end – the judgement – we are told will be sudden. We do not know the cumulative effect of the strains which we are placing on the world's system. We cannot foretell whether it is just running down or whether there is a breaking point or, if there is, when it will be. It is only by gaining a new vision, for as the Psalmist said: 'Without vision the people perish'. We have to rekindle a sense of urgency and a longing for a New Creation so that we are able to reorder our present priorities and promote the courageous actions which are necessary.

Christians believe that God created Man to have creative and moral capacities, which are meant to reflect God's own image. Because we have these gifts of God, we have both a natural inclination, and a duty, to understand the works of God, and to order our vocation accordingly. Our ability to make moral judgements affects our actions. We are answerable to God for all that we do, and every action should be taken with a sense of awe and deep humility at the wonderful works of God's Creation of which we are but a part.

The Early Church

Many of the saints had an attitude of reverence and respect for nature because they were servants of God, and nature was God's handiwork, and they were an integral part of that handiwork. Bede in his life of St Cuthbert wrote: 'It is hardly strange that the rest of Creation should obey the wishes and commands of a man who has dedicated himself with complete sincerity to the Lord's service. We, on the other hand, often lose that dominion over creation which is ours by right, through neglecting to serve its Creator.'

St Isaac the Syrian asked: 'What is a charitable heart?' 'It is a heart which is burning with charity for the whole of creation, for men, for the birds, for the beasts, for the demons – for all creatures. He who has such a heart cannot see or call to mind a creature without his eyes being filled with tears by reason of the immense compassion which seizes his heart.' Athanasius in his life of St Anthony pointed out how the saint lived in harmony with all nature, including crocodiles and olive trees. St Martin of

Tours, generally shown as sharing his soldier's cloak with a beggar, was also in harmony with animal life. A Christian shares the earth with all other living creatures, and if he is compassionate towards other forms of life, he will be in harmony with his fellow men. Kevin of Glendelough in Ireland (AD 618) refused an offer to build a monastery on the Wicklow hills on the grounds that 'I have no wish that the creatures of God should be moved because of me. Moreover, all the wild creatures on these mountains are my housemates, gentle and familiar with me, and they would be sad.'

St Francis of Assisi by his life and example drew Christian attention to the love of animals, and much Christian concern for nature has centred on a sentimental regard for birds and animals. St Catharine of Siena said that the reason why God's servants love His creatures so deeply is that they realize how deeply Christ loves them. This love needs to be extended beyond the care of individual animals to the conservation of whole species. It is not necessary to be cruel or to kill animals in order to threaten the survival of a species. If we destroy, pollute or possess their natural habitat, or interfere with their migratory patterns or breeding areas, the future of a species can be put at risk. Christians have a moral duty not to deny the chance of survival of a particular species, just as much as an individual animal. But the threat to the natural order today is much wider than the extinction of threatened plant and animal species. This is but a symptom of our treatment of all things.

Albert of Cologne, Archbishop of Ratisbon, known as Albert the Great, was a Dominican who observed nature in all its forms, reflecting on the knowledge revealed by the science and philosophy of the Greeks and Arabs, which had by then come into Western Europe like intellectual dynamite. He wrote: 'The aim of natural science is not simply to accept the statements of others, but to investigate the causes that are at work in Nature.' One of Albert's pupils was Roger Bacon who, with Robert Grosseteste, then Bishop of Lincoln, was perhaps one of the founding fathers of a Christian experimental study of nature. Bacon claimed that Christians had a duty to inquire as part of the 'Amor intellectus Dei', the duty to love God with all the mind. Our technology arises from this application of knowledge to secure the means to serve human needs, and it still offers the best hope of serving environmental ends. What is lacking is the moral strength to assess the varying values of the different options offered by technology.

More Recent Times

The recent concern of the Christian Church has tended to reflect a view that creation exists for humanity's sole benefit. This was justified by the interpretation of the command in Genesis 'to have dominion over the earth', as freedom to exploit it. The Industrial Revolution gave this utilitarian and instrumental view of nature a considerable boost.

The Archbishop of Canterbury, Dr R. Runcie, has said: 'When we are beginning to appreciate the wholeness and inter-relatedness of all that is in the cosmos, preoccupation with humanity can seem distinctly parochial. We need now to extend the area of the sacred and not to reduce it. The non-human parts of creation [should] be seen as having an intrinsic value of their own, rather than being dependent for value on their relation to human beings.'

Many people within the other main religious faiths of the world see Christian attitudes, especially in the Western Church, as being largely responsible for the degradation of the environment. The accusation is levelled at Christianity that our sense of dominion over Creation and the aggressive thrust of our western economic attitudes has been the cause of the ruthless exploitation of natural resources with all its consequent problems. But there was a time before Christianity when the north African deserts were the bread basket of the then known world. The Roman Empire, as well as many other ancient civilizations, was as ruthless as any modern exploiter. This suggests that it is in human nature to look after our short-term self-interest, but there is sufficient truth in the accusation for Christians to be particularly humble in their response to the contemporary degradation of the natural environment.

Darwin's theories about evolution seemed to challenge the authority of both scripture and tradition. Unfortunately the popular interpretation of his theory was that it was a matter of 'the survival of the fittest'. It was further misconstrued to apply to socio-economic arguments. The language of competition, survival, free market, dominance, protection, self-interest, became common currency in the value system of international trade, business and politics. With this view came the implication that the world is a basically competitive environment and that survival for both the individual and the group has to be a major preoccupation, and can only be achieved at the expense of other individuals or groups.

Schweitzer considered that reverence for life is the 'fundamental principle of ethics', and he saw no qualitative difference between human and animal life, so that all life is sacred, and commands that degree of respect. Teilhard de Chardin pointed out that Man made in the image of God exercises a dominion that is one of responsibility and duty to the environment. Sin alienates us from God and causes us to reject the spiritual values which underpin our trust of dominion. It is a delicate balance of order between humanity and nature, which does not deify nature, nor must it exaggerate the sanctity of life at one extreme or human ability at the other. Moltmann describes our relationship with Creation as one of fellowship. Jesus came to serve rather than be served, 'and he served in order to make us for fellowship with God and openness for one another'. In the light of Christ's mission Genesis 1.28 has to be interpreted, not as 'subdue the earth', but as 'free the earth through fellowship with it'. In his 1985 Gifford Lectures, Moltmann pointed out that the climax of God's act of Creation in Genesis was not the forming of Adam, but the seventh day when God rested and the whole of His Creation was living together.

When we work for a policy of fitting into the whole, we are working with the grain of all existence. It is the Doctrine of Exchange which was a central theme in the novels, poetry and theology of Charles Williams, and has been taken up by the Roman Catholic lay theologian, Rosemary Haughton. As fellow creatures of this one world we depend on one another for everything and are responsible for one another in everything. We live, therefore, in a continuous exchange of care and support and service and, indeed, life. Most of the time it is not caused by any deliberate philanthropy on our part but is, rather, inherent in the very nature of things.

THE APPEAL TO REASON
AND EXPERIENCE

Bishop John Taylor has pointed out that the kaleidoscopic set of Christian attitudes towards nature over the ages is not a cause for pessimism, for it is the function of a kaleidoscope to turn disorder into symmetry and to make a pattern out of confusion. Any Christian attitude does demand that we survey our attitudes from many angles for truth is many-faceted.

Man's dominion over nature is a limited one in which the exercise of authority is balanced by a duty to protect, conserve and foster. So we have duties in relation to our exercise of power. In respect to the living world, we are, like many other species in the natural order, a predator. This places upon us a duty to use our liberty responsibly. We are not given a licence to abuse. Pain is part of the natural order, but it is an abuse of power wantonly to inflict pain. The infliction of pain is wanton when it has no morally convincing reason.

We have a moral duty not to put at risk the chances of survival of other species by our own actions, on the religious ground that every species is an inherent part of God's Creation towards which we owe a sense of responsibility. We need humility in our approach to progress and development and the wisdom to understand and foresee the consequences of our own actions, if we are not to destroy or disturb such a delicately interdependent system as the biosphere.

The Christian attitude to nature can best be expressed through three images which run both through the Scriptures and the tradition of the Church, and which have been pointed out in a recent publication of the Church of Scotland, *While the Earth Endures* (p.19):

1. We are Stewards of God's Creation. Stewardship implies the manner in which we treat the world around us. A Steward does not ruthlessly exploit or exhaust the resources entrusted to him. He does not shelve or try to

shift his responsibility for any situation, nor let it grow worse through neglect. He thinks not solely in terms of the present but has a responsibility for the future.

2. We are Custodians or Trustees of God's Creation. A Trustee holds his trust because he is responsible. It means leaving the inheritance in at least as good a condition as he received it and, if possible, in an enhanced state for the future. No person worthy of trust will abuse that confidence by allowing his trust to be degraded, neglected or reduced to ugliness.

3. We are Companions. Companionship expresses the interdependence of each constituent part. We co-exist and share our world together. 'The role of companion excluded the possibility of adversarial tactics with nature – that attitude of confrontation and control which was thought until recently to be an essential part of "the scientific method".'

The Value of Nature

If nature is to command human respect, and to be worthy of it, we must believe that it possesses certain values. For the Christian the first value is inherent and lies in the belief that the whole cosmos is a part of God's handiwork and responsibility and, therefore, commands our respect as being 'of God'.

The second value is instrumental and is one of self-interest. The practical necessity for Christians to care for the cosmos is clear, because our future existence and that of our children depends upon the well-being of the living world of which we are an interdependent part. Self-preservation is a powerful argument. If man does not conserve the natural environment and seek to repair the damage which he is doing, he will destroy the very means on which he depends for his existence. The moral argument of self-interest is a necessary and practical one, but it is not sufficient in itself because it does not go far enough. If man can often be relied upon to do the right thing in the end, so often, unfortunately, it is only when he has exhausted every other possible alternative. In many cases so much irreversible and irreparable damage has been done that the final state is poorer than the first.

The human spirit is unique in being able to feel and to express its awe of the natural environment. The beauties and wonders of our natural environment nourish our spiritual senses, and have been the inspiration for much of our art, music, drama and poetry, as well as providing refreshment and recreation for the human spirit. Areas of wilderness have always had a special fascination for men and women as places of primitive beauty and struggle, but where we also experience the deepest feelings of the human spirit, and come very close to God. 'Consider the lilies, even Solomon in all his glory was not arrayed like one of these.' (Luke 12.27).

Professor Victor Weisskopf has said: 'Those first days have been depicted in various forms, in pictures and poetry, but to me, Franz Josef Haydn's oratorio *The Creation* is the most remarkable rendition of the Big Bang. At the beginning we hear a choir of angels singing mysteriously and softly, "And God said Let there be Light". And at the words "And there was Light" the entire choir and the orchestra explode into a blazing impressive presentation of the beginning of everything.'

Fourthly, nature has an intrinsic value of its own. If we, as Christians, believe that God made animals, plants, mountains, oceans and rivers, as well as human beings, then all those created things must have a value in their own right. They then acquire a moral standing, even though they are incapable of representing their own interests. And that has to be taken into consideration, in the same way that we should allow for the interests of a child or a senile person, who is not capable of representing himself. Indeed, the inability of the natural order to represent itself places upon humans an even greater responsibility to take it into consideration and care for its needs. God is love and sees His Creation as good; the love extends to the whole of that Creation and He must desire good not only for the human part of His Creation, but the whole of it. 'Are not two sparrows sold for a farthing? And not one of them shall fall on the ground without your Father' knowing. (Matthew 10.29).

The sacredness of life cannot be all-embracing. There are various levels of value and some parts of nature are accorded greater value by humans than others. There are, for instance, various bacteria, viruses, etc., against which we perceive that we have a responsibility to protect both humanity and animals, and these will confront us with a conflict of duties which we have to work out, by our moral reason, in a responsible balance. But the difficult moral problems do not usually lie with such direct issues, but between competing claims, when each has a degree of reason and legitimacy. Both seals and humans eat fish, and they are competing for the dwindling stocks in the oceans; what is the right answer? Within the natural world the ecological balance is maintained by a certain level of predation. There are plenty of predators, but none so indiscriminate as man. Rarity often gives added value and can enhance the need for conservation. But in all these value judgements our anthropocentric attitudes create a system whereby these judgements are heavily influenced by the extent of their usefulness or attractiveness to man.

Science and Technology

In modern times man has come to believe implicitly in the power of science and in the technology that has developed from scientific knowledge. A strong belief in the beneficent potential of science and technology is acceptable, provided it is exercised with wisdom and foresight. Creation, seen as there simply to be exploited by man for the use of man, leads to the creation of organizations as bureaucracies, and this tends to transform human existence from being organic to being something organized. Such organizations are too often materialistic and human centred to the exclusion of God and of spiritual values. However, science and technology, rightly used, also offer us the best hope for redressing errors of human judgement and abuses of the natural environment.

As science and technology are the domain of inquiring minds, so theology has to rediscover a similar sense of exploration. As man is both material and spiritual, his search for wisdom and for God has to be related to an understanding of our contemporary experience.

Man has a responsibility to the future as well as to the present. This generation is only able to enjoy its standard of living as a result of the efforts of past generations who built for the future. We have a moral responsibility to hold in trust that which we have received, to add value to our inheritance to the best of our ability so as to pass on to the future an enriched inheritance. The Parable of the Talents makes our Christian duty clear. No single generation should act so selfishly or exploit resources so ruthlessly that the future is mortgaged and we pass on an impoverished heritage.

Marx and Engels wrote in their *Manifesto*: 'The bourgeois has subjected the country to the rule of the town. It has created enormous cities, has greatly increased the urban population as compared with the rural and has thus rescued part of the population from the idiocy of rural life.' Both Marx and Adam Smith regarded nature purely as a store supplying the raw materials for the transformation of human society. Schumacher commented of modern urban man: 'Modern man does not experience himself as part of nature, but as an outside force destined to dominate and conquer it. He even talks of a battle with nature, forgetting that if ever he won the battle, he would find himself on the losing side.'

Western civilization has become locked into an economic system that thrives on more and more material growth; its justification is to produce more and more things for more and more people. The level of living standard enjoyed by countries like America, Japan and much of Europe is never likely to be realized by the other eighty percent of the world's population. Solutions may require a form of redistribution, which could demand self-denial and unselfishness from those who have much, for Jesus said (Luke 14.28): 'To whomsoever much is given, much shall be required.'

The population of the world is growing at a faster rate than the natural system is likely to be able to support, and the fastest growth is in those underdeveloped areas least able to sustain such increase.

The twin problems of unlimited economic growth in the richer countries, combined with the exponential growth of population in the poorer countries, raises for Christians many issues of Justice. The economic order for Christians has not only got to be sustainable, but its effects must be just and seen to be just. But, as the Brundtland Commission has pointed out, sustainable growth with justice is within our grasp, and our hope can lie in the right use of science and technology. We have the resources, what is lacking is the will.

Christians need to be challenged to think about difficult problems in a new light. We have to stop being obsessed with ourselves and our humanity. We need to strive for quality, rather than quantity. The depth of our altruistic concern is a measure of our spiritual maturity.

COMING TO A DECISION

There will be occasions when a clear decision can be taken by the Christian on moral and ethical grounds. There will be many others where there are competing interests, and where the good to be achieved and the cost to be paid have to be carefully weighed. Judgement is always a question of balance. The Christian has to use his understanding to weigh the competing values of the interests concerned and make his judgement on the grounds of his moral principles.

The Christian has a moral duty

1. to understand his situation within the earth's biosphere, and the situation of the earth in space;
2. to understand the good to be attempted and the evil to be averted in all his judgements;
3. to consider the means to be adopted and the consequences for good and bad of his actions, actual and potential;
4. to balance the possible benefits against the risks of his decisions.

For the Christian that moral obligation rests on the belief:

(a) that this is God's Creation;

(b) that Humanity is an interdependent part of that Creation;

(c) that, under God, the Christian has a moral obligation to understand his own position within that Creation. His 'dominion' over nature can only be seen in terms of a custodianship, a tenancy, which he holds in trust for the future;

(d) that the Christian must recognize his own limitations, and he interferes with the immensity, complexity and delicate balance of the Creation at his own peril;

(e) that pride, ignorance and selfishness are the greatest obstacles, whilst knowledge, understanding and wisdom are the greatest assets;

(f) that the Christian has a moral obligation to strive for justice and salvation, which is not restricted to humanity, but which includes the whole of God's Creation.

The Christian attitude to nature is based upon the conviction that the whole cosmos is the creation of God and, therefore, we humans have a duty to respect it as such with reverence and in the realization that we are but tenants in our lifetime. It is our responsibility in our generation to see that the inheritance which has come to us is handed on to our successors in at least as good a state as we received it.

We need to see our actions as being morally right. We all need to believe in what we are doing. The Christian faith is inspired by the belief that God so loved His world that He became a man in the person of Jesus Christ, who not only set us an example of how we should live but also gives us the grace, through the power of the Holy Spirit, to live up to the standards which He has set.

The Christian needs to recognize the practical reasons to care for the natural environment, and he requires the moral reasons to assure him that it is right and also God's will. If we ignore the moral and practical reasons, the wheel will come full circle. A continuing failure to respond responsibly, will destroy the very Creation on which we depend for our existence. So the moral and pragmatic arguments interlock.

In Galatians 5.22–24 St Paul lists nine fruits of the Spirit, which might be used for a Christian attitude to nature:

1. **Love** – for the whole of God's Creation. We humans are not as important as we would like to think. We need to move away from self-love towards altruism, and from anthropocentric attitudes towards ecocentric ones.

2. **Joy** – in God's Creation.

3. **Peace** – with God's Creation. If humanity were in harmony with itself, it would be in harmony with nature.

4. **Patience** – with the natural process and sensitivity to its requirements.

5. **Kindness**, (**and** 6. **Goodness**) – living respectfully with nature. In our responsibility for custodianship of the world, in the practice of our trusteeship in all aspects of our lives, and in concern for the consequences of our actions.

7. **Faithfulness** – in our responsibility for our stewardship of the Creation, and in the practice of our trusteeship in all aspects of our lives.

8. **Humility** – in our ambition for material progress and the exercise of our scientific and technological powers.

[67]

9. **Self-control** – restraint in our demands upon our environment and its resources. Greed and selfishness have to be curbed because they have become excessive and, therefore, evil.

APPENDICES

APPENDIX A

Attitude Studies

Those who attended the seven consultations at St George's House, Windsor Castle, produced a number of 'Attitude Studies', which raise questions about our response to certain issues. They try to apply theological insights to specific problems. At this stage, they often raise more questions than they answer and these questions provoke much thought, and demand further discussion before right answers are likely to be found. They are the result of some of the thought given to this topic over the seven consultations, and are not the responsibility of the joint authors of this book, but they do indicate and illustrate the way in which Christians might be thinking, although we may disagree with particular propositions or solutions.

AGEING

One of the factors in the human population is that we are able to keep more and more people alive for longer and longer. Any consideration of this issue must start with the Christian view of the sanctity of life as being God-given. However, the human purpose in living an earthly life should not be to prolong it at all costs, for to Christians who believe in a life hereafter, that would be a fundamentally un-Christian attitude.

The Bible suggests that there is a natural span to life (threescore years and ten). Modern medicine aided by technology is often able to extend that natural span. Because of the great difficulties and dangers inherent in any departure from the principle of keeping life going at any cost, all the pressures, until very recently, have been towards 'officiously striving to keep alive'.

Christians have a duty to think through and pray about this issue more deeply. The Hospice Movement has stirred new signs of hope, in helping people to die with dignity and even with joy. The emphasis has been a Christian one of surrounding the dying with love and creating an atmosphere of peace and acceptance, rather than a strict adherence to the prolongation of life. Does this imply the right, in terminal illness, to alleviate pain and distress, even when the cost and the side effect may be that death is not postponed for as long as might be technically possible?

This also raises the question whether the quality of life is just as important as the quantity of days, especially for those whose hope is one of eternal life.

BIOTECHNOLOGY:

The major moral and ethical issue of the late twentieth century

Biotechnology and genetic engineering hold out the promise to resolve many of the environmental and pollution problems we have been discussing:

— over the next twenty years land will become thirty to fifty percent more productive than at present;
— this could be achieved with the help of crops that do not

need fertilizers and pesticide inputs and so will cause less pollution;

— in poorer countries, crops will be able to be grown in areas that are too dry or too saline to support agriculture at the moment;

— safer and more effective drugs will be produced in crops, animals and microbiol culture, rather than in factories and laboratories;

— micro-organisms will be developed to break down complex pollutants and to concentrate minerals from low-grade ores and mine tailings in commercial quantities;

— some micro-organisms will be able to increase the yield of oil from oil wells and others will be able to synthesize high-grade oils in commercial quantities;

— hereditary diseases will be curable by gene therapy involving manipulation *in vitro* of the human embryo;

— we will have more effective vaccines, some for diseases not now controllable in this way, without inflicting suffering on animals as at present.

Reassurances: The Arguments

These new developments will allow us to keep our present standards of living, and even to continue to grow, and at the same time to improve the environment. Many developments will benefit poorer countries. It is often claimed that we have been engaging in biotechnology for centuries, bread and wine are products of biotechnology, and have not come to any harm. Farm animal breeds have been improved by genetic selection over the centuries. We are only talking about an increase in the scale of activity, not in the fundamental nature of the activity.

Risks: The Arguments

Past experience shows that micro-organisms can get out of control in the environment and create havoc, myxomatosis, dutch elm disease. Some commercial developments of biotechnology may not be environmentally benign, e.g. the development of herbicide-resistant crops where farmers will be able to spray heavy doses of herbicide and make land suitable only to grow varieties of crops produced by the herbicide manufacturer. Increases in land productivity will create social disruption on a major scale. What will happen if thirty percent of European rural land is no longer needed for agriculture? Even if this land is used to benefit conservation, there will be adverse impacts on the people living there.

However, biotechnology is the first example of a technological advance that is being subjected to pro-active risk regulation, we are attempting, at government and international levels, to anticipate the hazards and regulate for them (e.g. any micro-organism released into the environment must be incapable of long-term persistence in the environment).

Ethics: The Arguments

Any developments that involve genetic manipulation raise serious ethical questions and lead to accusations of 'playing God'. In the past we have relied on natural variation followed by selection, for desirable characteristics, and have no moral problems with this. Our new ability to insert genes from one species into the chromosomes of another in order to produce a characteristic which we desire, for commercial purposes, is *not* just more of the same. It needs to be rethought from the ethical viewpoint.

Have we the right to manipulate other micro-organisms, plants and animals, for our own ends, in this way? If we have, does it apply to all three categories, i.e. does it include plants but not animals, or does it include the human species?

Is there a line to be drawn? If so, its drawing is an ethical and moral issue.

Where are the boundaries between our duty to care for God's Creation and to develop its full potential, and the injunction not to meddle with or change what has been created?

ENVIRONMENTAL IMPACT OF HUMAN ACTIVITIES

Attention has been drawn recently to the global warming of the earth, what has been called the greenhouse effect. There is growing evidence of a number of causes, among them the release of carbon dioxide and nitrous oxide into the atmosphere from desertification, the burning of fossil fuels, and of the destruction of the rain forests. Scientists warn us that the increase of air pollution may bring about an increase in the temperature, which could, in turn cause a melting of the ice-cap and consequent flooding to low-lying areas as the level of the oceans rise. Such a threat is particularly serious for countries like Holland and Bangladesh and areas such as East Anglia.

A great deal can be done to alleviate the worst effects of air pollution: (1) It is important to maintain our vegetation cover by preserving the tropical rain forest, and forests in temperate zones all of which help to absorb carbon dioxide. (2) We need to reduce the burning of fossil fuel, by conserving energy through more effective insulation and more efficient engines, and the more careful use of existing sources of energy. (3) Nuclear power and the development of alternative sources of energy can achieve great savings in air pollution. A failure to pursue these courses may involve an enormous outlay of resources in building flood barriers, and even in having to resettle on higher ground.

If the Christian sees his attitude to the earth as being one of steward, trustee and companion, he will:

(a) want to leave his inheritance in at least as good a state as he inherited it;

(b) feel it irresponsible to shrug off problems to which we have contributed, and leave them for our children to face;

(c) encourage any step that will husband, conserve and enhance our heritage;

(d) take any practical measures open to him, no matter how small the scale, both in his personal life and by bringing pressure to bear on those who have the power to effect change;

(e) consider whether a more simple form of lifestyle may be appropriate.

The Christian is faced with three alternatives:

1. Wait and see, as scientists are still uncertain.

2. Leave it to posterity, as nothing is likely to happen for fifty years.

3. Act now, taking into consideration the social consequences of limiting the exploitation of natural resources by the rural poor in the less developed countries.

DIVERSITY OF NATURE

The living world can be likened to a living organism. What was created is an ever changing system, held in dynamic equilibrium by constant adjustment and fine tuning by the inexorable laws of Nature.

Individual parts of the system become redundant, wither and die – new parts are generated; their creation stimulated by small changes in the weather or climate and the tensions within the system.

Change and adaptation are normal – all is connected – Creation is a whole.

The changes that do occur take place over millions of years except where natural catastrophes, both small and large, occur – or where man is involved. When such events happen the very diverse but interlinked nature of Creation provides the means to repair the damage that has been inflicted on Creation.

To make clear the time scales of evolution and destruction it has become popular to compare the life of the universe to a human year. If this is so then a day lasts ten million years, and an hour over 400,000 years. On such a timescale, evolution produced the first alga in August, the first marine forms in the second week of November, fish a week later, and the first lizard not until the middle of December. Man does not appear until late in the evening of the 31st December, the final day. Industrial man appears only two seconds from midnight. On this reckoning, the next fifty-seven years last half a second.

Yet in that time man is expected to eliminate a third or more of all species on earth: diversity which has taken since the beginning of biological time to evolve. This is an accomplishment our generation will be remembered for, an accomplishment which has brought greater disorder to God's Creation than any natural disaster.

Of all the species linked together in this close knit mesh which is God's Creation, under two million species have been closely studied and there are probably at least thirty million. All but a few thousand are at risk. In a dynamic system, change, decay, extinction, evolution and new birth is ever present. The Christian responsibility is to ensure that human activities are not the cause of damage or degredation to the earth's biosphere.

POPULATION

The moral dilemma confronting Christians lies in our reverence for life on the one hand, and the practical need to curb population on the other. We add to our population at the rate of 150 a minute, or 85,000,000 a year. The increase has been made possible by man's ability to control death (infant mortality, and medicine both curative and preventative). Ninety percent of the growth is in the poorer countries and it is concentrated in cities, where slums abound and existence is undernourished and without dignity. The fertility boom will change the structure of many societies and will raise severe problems of dependency and political instability due to the predominance of young people in the total population.

Whilst parents have the right to decide upon the number of children they wish to have, they have a responsibility to take all considerations into account. The disagreement among Christians arises over the methods that may or may not be used to control fertility.

Although fertility is not easy to control, there are some factors which give grounds for hope:

1. the age of marriage;
2. the extent of breast feeding;
3. the prevalence of contraception;
4. the extent of abortion.

Christians will have no difficulty in agreeing to support

and encourage action under the first two headings, but they are completely divided on the last two.

If the core of the problem facing the world lies in population growth, the core of that problem lies in the education of women. In many countries children are seen as a means of labour, of status, and an insurance against old age. However, more children involve greater expense to parents and to society in providing housing, clothing, food, health care and education. Christians need to strive for alternative options in these societies so that the needs to provide employment opportunities for the young and an economic wage and security in old age can be met by other means within the structure of the local society.

Christians must press for the continuing education of girls and women, especially in their relationships with their husbands, and the many women's organizations could provide an excellent forum for such education. The Church has a major role to play in educating both men and women through its own network of organizations. Women need to be made aware of options open to them other than child bearing. It must be the Christian view that any limitation in child bearing should be entirely voluntary. We need to remember that there are now more Christians in the developing world than in the affluent world.

Christians in Britain need to press for a re-examination of the theology of marriage, so that more emphasis can be placed on loving relationships and less on procreation, together with the removal of economic inducements to remain single or to become one-parent families. The present divisions within Christianity prevent us from speaking in a credible manner about population growth because of our inability to come to a common mind over the theological implications of family planning through contraception and abortion. The division of opinion over the use of many forms of contraception seriously weakens the Christian witness, especially as the rules laid down by some churches are observed more in the breach than the observance. Christians need to press for more ecumenical dialogue on the status of Christian marriage, and no serious inter-faith dialogue on family life is possible until this is done.

There is a need for more political will and more research in order to achieve a level of sustainable population. We have the resources but do not show either the religious or political will to deploy them, in view of the changes of attitude needed and the costs that would be required.

Population growth which goes beyond the supportive capacity of the land, or beyond the planning capacities of governments, aggravates all environmental problems. Damaging the environment reinforces the poverty of the poorest people, among whom birth rates are highest.

MAKING DEVELOPMENT SUSTAINABLE

Do we need growth?

Economic growth has become a basic concept in human society. It enables the developed countries to have the high standards of living they enjoy. It is the only mechanism available to alleviate the poverty of many parts of the developing world. To renounce growth altogether is to remove from many people any hope of a better future.

Will any growth do?

But a main message of this book is that some kinds of economic growth cannot be sustained on a planet of limited size and with limited mineral and biological resources. The planet has finite resources. They can be squandered. The exploitation of resources of all sorts needs to be sustainable.

So the solution must lie in reconciling the need for growth with the need for conserving and, indeed, improving the planet's resources. This means planning for development which meets the needs of the present without compromising the ability of future generations to meet their own needs. This is sustainable development, as recommended by the Brundtland Commission. The challenge that now faces us is how to achieve sustainable development in practice.

Making development sustainable

The implications of making development sustainable affect thinking at many levels.

At the global level, countries need to undertake to work together to this end, and to renounce policies that simply reflect their own interests. The Brundtland report has started this process. The big global issues of ozone depletion and climate change have shown the indispensability of action on a global scale.

At the national level, the need is for sustainability to be taken into account in all areas of economic policy making. This introduces a new dimension into decision taking. It means working on a much longer time-scale than we often do. And it means assessing the effect of development proposals on renewable natural resources. Developing methods of measurement here is difficult but essential. It will require analysis of the qualitative nature of development as well as its conventional economic benefit.

[81]

Some examples of the effects of sustainability at topic level are:

(a) The need to avoid over-fishing so that stocks are preserved.

(b) The need to conserve tropical rainforests in order to provide timber for future generations, and also to preserve the species diversity found in the forests and of which future generations may be able to make better use than ourselves.

(c) The overriding need to use energy in the most efficient way, with the optimum use of primary energy sources (including renewable sources, sun, wind, water, etc.). The analysis must take proper account of environmental issues such as acid rain, the greenhouse effect and disposal of radioactive wastes. And because energy is so major a user of renewable resources in the less developed countries, we must be as sparing in its use as we can, meaning developing new habits of energy conservation.

(d) Waste should be minimized and, whenever possible, recycled. It is often an unwanted product rather than a dangerous enemy.

(e) Looking carefully at proposals for altering traditional methods of agriculture and land management, particularly where new methods involve major use of irrigation and chemical fertilizers or pesticides.

The Christian view

For the policy maker, sustainability means reaching decisions within a much broader framework of space and time, and within an economic system which turns all the costs and benefits into accounts.

But for the Christian, sustainability means a responsible expression of stewardship of God's Creation; and a proper working out in practice of love for his brother both born and as yet unborn.

APPENDIX B

A List of Participants

The Christian Attitude to Nature

Her Grace The Duchess of Abercorn Counsellor in Transpersonal Psychology.

Mr George Barrett Head of Policy, Corporate Environment, CEGB.

Dr Andrew Basden Frodsham Evangelical Fellowship; Green Party; Lecturer in Information Technology, Salford University.

Mrs Angela Beer School teacher.

Mr Ian Beer Head Master, Harrow School.

Professor R. J. Berry Professor of Genetics; President, British Ecological Society.

Mr J. Truman Bidwell, Jr. Attorney-at-law, New York.

Mr Christopher Bowers IBM Corporate Programmes.

Mrs Nita Bowers Housewife.

Mrs Margaret Bright Housewife.

Mr Peter Bright External Affairs Division (Environmental Issues), Shell International Petroleum Company Limited.

Professor Neville Brown Professor of International Security Affairs, University of Birmingham.

Mrs Audrey T. Bryant Joint National Co-ordinator, Christian Ecology Group.

The Lord Buxton Chairman, Anglia TV; Survival Anglia.

The Revd Dr Brian Chalmers Senior Chaplain, University of Kent, Canterbury.

Mrs Judith Chalmers Teacher.

Dr Roger Clarke Director – Policy, Countryside Commission.

The Rt Revd Peter Coleman Bishop of Crediton.

The Revd Dr Geoffrey M. W. Cook Vice-Master, St Edmund's College, Cambridge; research biochemist; deacon of the Roman Catholic Church.

Mr Tim Cooper National Co-ordinator, Christian Ecology Group, 1981–85; freelance economist/environmental consultant.

Mrs Barbara Cousins Religious consultant, International Consultancy on Religion, Education and Culture (ICOREC).

Mr John Davidson Chief Executive, Groundwork Foundation.

Miss M. Eve Dennis Development Officer, Church and Conservation Project, Arthur Rank Centre.

Professor The Revd Gordon Dunstan Honorary Research Fellow, University of Exeter.

Mrs Barbara Echlin Teacher.

Dr Edward P. Echlin Theologian.

His Royal Highness The Duke of Edinburgh, KG.

Dr John M. Edington Director of Environmental Studies, University of Wales.

Dr M. Ann Edington Bacteriologist.

Dr Michael M. Edwards Director of Academic Affairs, Middlesex Polytechnic.

Dr D. J. Fisk Chief Scientist, Department of the Environment.

Mrs Eileen Francis Head, Enterprise in Education, Moray House College, Edinburgh.

Dr John M. Francis Director Scotland, Nature Conservancy Council; Chairman, Society, Religion and Technology Project, Church of Scotland.

Mrs Rosalind Gilmore Directing Fellow, St George's House.

Mrs Hannah Gosling.

The Revd Dr John Gosling Research Fellow.

Sir Peter Harrop Formerly Department of the Environment.

Mr Ivan Hattingh Biologist; World Wide Fund for Nature, UK.

Mr Ronald Higgins Director of Dunamis, St James's Church, Piccadilly; author of *The Seventh Enemy*, etc.

Mr John Hobson Director, Central Directorate of Environmental Protection, Department of the Environment.

Mr Peter Holden Education Department, Royal Society for the Protection of Birds.

The Revd Friar Peter Hooper, OFM   Roman Catholic friar-
    priest; Lecturer in Liturgy; Principal of Franciscan Study
    Centre, Canterbury.
Professor Christopher Howes   Director of Land and Property
    Division, Department of the Environment.
The Revd Keith Innes   Rector of Alfold and Loxwood; author of
    Grove Ethical Study *Caring for the Earth*.
Wing Cdr A. G. Trevenen James   Vice Chairman, Population
    Concern.
Mr Pieter Kuipers   Director P.D. Consumer Electronics, Philips
    International BV, The Netherlands.
Dr Derek Langslow   Nature Conservancy Council.
Mr Hugh Locke   Deputy Director, Baha'i International Com-
    munity's Office of Public Information.
Professor James Lovelock, FRS   Independent scientist.
Sir William McCrea, FRS   Emeritus Professor of Astronomy,
    University of Sussex.
Mr John Malleson   Secretary of the Ernest Cook Trust.
Mrs Judy Malleson   Awards Assistant, Ernest Cook Trust.
The Rt Revd Michael Mann   Dean of Windsor.
The Revd Jeremy Martineau   Joint Secretary, ACORA; Chair-
    man, ACRE.
Dr Peter Mayhew   Conservation Officer, British Association
    for Shooting and Conservation.
The Very Revd Patrick R. Mitchell   Dean of Wells.
Dr Janet Moore   College Lecturer, Cambridge; biologist.
Dr Norman Moore   Chief Advisory Officer, Nature Conser-
    vancy Council (retired); Biologist.
Mr Tim O'Donovan   Trustee, The Environment Foundation;
    Chairman, Better Environment Awards for Industry Man-
    agement Committee.
Mr Martin Palmer   Director, ICOREC; Religious Advisor to
    World Wide Fund for Nature, UK.
Mrs Sandra Palmer   Lecturer in Religious Studies.
Mr Derek G. Pearce   Farmer; Business Consultant; Chairman,
    Outside Directors Ltd.
Mrs Nancy Pearce   Founder Chairman, Anorexic Family Aid.
Mr Claude D. Pike, OBE, DL   Industry; dendrology; woodland
    owner.
The Revd Dr John Rodwell   Ecologist, University of Lancaster.

The Revd Canon John Rogan Director, Bristol Board of Social
   Responsibility.
Mrs Margaret Rogan Housewife.
Mr John Rowley Editor, *People* Magazine.
Mr Michael Shackleton Head of English Studies, Osaka
   Gakuin University; part-time Consultant, ICOREC.
Mr Jim Shelley Secretary to The Church Commissioners.
Mr Roger Shorter Green Discipleship Group.
Mrs Libushka Smart.
Professor Ninian Smart Professor of Religious Studies, Uni-
   versity of California and Lancaster University.
Mr Edward Smith, CB Deputy Secretary, Ministry of
   Agriculture; Member, Archbishops' Commission on Rural
   Areas.
The Revd Canon Derek Stanesby Canon of Windsor.
The Lord Swann, FRS.
The Lady Swann.
Dr Alex D. Tait Lecturer, Cambridge University.
Dr E. Joyce Tait Senior Lecturer, Open University.
Mr Colin Taylor Marine biologist, CEGB.
The Rt Revd John Taylor Retired Bishop of Winchester.
Mr Robert Troake Manager, Technical Services Division,
   Group Environmental Services, BP International Ltd.
The Revd Canon W. H. Vanstone Canon Residentiary of
   Chesterr Cathedral.
Sir Ralph Verney, KBE Past Chairman, Nature Conservancy
   Council.
Lady Verney Musician.
Mr R. Bradman Weerakoon Secretary-General, International
   Planned Parenthood Federation.
His Grace The Duke of Wellington, LVO, OBE, MC, DL
   Landowner and farmer.
Mr William H. N. Wilkinson Chairman, Nature Conservancy
   Council.
Mrs Hazel Wise Housewife.
The Very Revd Randolph Wise Dean of Peterborough.
Mrs Isolde Woolley, MAG.Phil. Linguist.
Mr G. Nicholas Woolley, FRICS, FAAV Director Administra-
   tion and Chief Land Agent, Prudential Portfolio Managers
   Limited, Property Division.

Mrs Anne M. G. Wyburd, JP Language teacher and translator.
Mr Giles Wyburd Director, ICC United Kingdom.

ST GEORGE'S HOUSE, WINDSOR CASTLE

ST GEORGE'S HOUSE, WINDSOR CASTLE

THE TRADITION AND PURPOSE OF THE HOUSE

In 1348 King Edward III founded the Order of the Garter, to consist of 26 noble knights, in his castle at Windsor. In the same year, and in the same place he created the ecclesiastical foundation of the College of St George with twenty-six priests. Two hundred years later, in the reign of Elizabeth I this College was required to add the task of learning to those of prayer and worship in its list of duties.

It was in this continuing historical tradition of the temporal, the spiritual and the reflective that St George's House was founded on that same site in the Castle of Windsor and was opened by Her Majesty the Queen on 23 October 1966.

St George's House sets out to do two tasks, each of which enlightens the other. These are:

1. To be a place where people of influence and responsibility in every area of society, e.g. in industry, commerce, the professions, politics, science, the arts and the Church, come together to explore, to develop and communicate, freely and frankly, their ideas and anxieties. It is a place where the values and standards of individuals and institutions can be brought into sharp focus and where the influence of spiritual experience on material affairs can be assessed and developed.

2. To be a place where clergy of all denominations can come together for short or long courses adapted to the needs of various stages of their career. Using the understanding gained in the total work of St George's House and calling on other knowledge and experience, the courses are designed to illuminate ministerial responsibility and functions in the context of modern conditions.

The life of Windsor Castle has a current relevance. It is a place where God continues to be worshipped. It is the residence of the Sovereign. It is a place where men and women of influence in our society meet to discuss the problems which confront them. It is this reality, this close relationship to current political, social, industrial and ecclesiastical problems and opportunities which provided the inspiration for those who founded the House. It continues to keep us, its current Council and staff, with our eyes firmly fixed on the immense problems and opportunities of late twentieth-century living.

The House consists physically of two Queen Anne houses situated behind St George's Chapel within the Castle walls. These houses have been converted to provide residential accommodation with twenty-four rooms. The 15th-century Chapter Library serves as the principal meeting room.

THE WORK OF THE HOUSE

In pursuit of its purpose, the work of the House falls into three categories:
The General Consultations, The Organization Consultations, The Clergy Courses and Consultations.
There are also a limited number of outside lettings.

The General Consultations

Each year the Council of the House reviews and selects those critical questions which are to be the concern of the House Topics include 'Science and Religion', 'The Divided Society?', 'Information Technology and Communication', 'Education to the Year 2000 and Beyond', and 'Citizenship, Income and Work'.

It is then the task of the Staff of the House to plan a series of consultations on these themes, seeking to bring together by invitation the different viewpoints on each part of the issue in question. The House provides the background staff work to the consultations, defining as best it can the precise nature of the questions and challenges that need to be faced in these consultations and the most appropriate way of presenting them.

These general consultations usually take place at the end of the week or over a weekend, lasting two days. Attendance is by invitation. A charge is made to cover the costs of accommodation. An Annual Lecture is delivered each year by a distinguished speaker to an invited audience in St George's Chapel.

The Organization Consultation

It is the policy of the House to work with a small number of large organizations to give their key people the time and means to reflect upon their values, aims and responsibilities in a changing society. In a meeting-place such as St George's, we can bring together people who will convey the kind of ideas and challenges which emerge both from the general consultations of the House and from the concerns of the organization itself.

These consultations normally last for the inside of a week and are jointly planned by the organization concerned and by the staff of the House.

The Clergy Courses and Consultations

It has always been an important part of the House's purpose to organize consultations for the leadership of Christian bodies of all denominations in which they might reflect upon their role and responsibilities amid the current challenges in society, in the belief that God is working his purpose out in this World. Almost half of the programme time of the House is devoted to this work.

Regular workshops and consultations on particular problems connected with the Churches are also organized. We seek to include representatives of all denominations although the greater number of participants come from the Anglican tradition.

FINANCIAL SUPPORT

The House is non-profit-making and largely self-supporting. The cost of the general consultations is just met by the modest accommodation fees charged to those who take part in them. The charges for the clergy courses are less than the cost, while the organization consultants yield a small surplus. But the overheads of the House and its staff are never fully met from its accommodation charges. Additional support comes from the

Associates of St George's House. We encourage those who have taken part in our consultations to join the Associates for a small annual subscription. This entitles them to regular information about the work of the House. They are invited to our Annual Lecture and this occasion also provides a way for the House to see again its many friends and associates. We are also supported by:

Corporate Associates

The House has a limited number of Corporate Associates. These are organizations who agree or covenant to support the work of the House for a specific term by a regular donation. They receive priority in arrangements for our organization consultations in addition to all the normal benefits of Associates.

We depend greatly on the goodwill of these Corporate Associates for our financial viability and we welcome enquiries.

BAIN CLARKSON LIMITED

Bain Clarkson Limited is an international insurance broking company with roots dating back to 1790. The company, a member of the Inchcape international marketing and services Group, is one of the four largest brokers of UK industrial and commercial business and ranks twelfth in the world. It has fifty subsidiary and associated outlets overseas and twenty-seven offices throughout the UK providing a comprehensive insurance, risk management, and independent financial planning service for corporate and private clients.

Bain Clarkson's client list includes Government ministries, State industries and utilities, as well as large to small businesses in manufacture, distribution, shipping, airlines, travel and transport. The Company has a specialized expertise in placing insurance for contractors, professional bodies and personal risks.

BAIN CLARKSON LIMITED

●

15 MINORIES
LONDON EC3N 1NJ
AND AT LLOYD'S
TELEPHONE: 01-481 3232
TELEX: 8813411 : FAX: 01-480 6137

A MEMBER OF THE INCHCAPE GROUP